CU00657848

The Art of
Talking to Strangers

Peter Spalton, The Dating Doctor ™

The Art of Talking to Strangers

First Published in January 2009 by

Peter Spalton
Suite 413, 27 Colmore Row
Birmingham B3 2EW
United Kingdom

help@thedatingdoctor.co.uk
www.thedatingdoctor.co.uk

Copyright © Peter Spalton 2009

All rights reserved.

No part of this publication may be reproduced, copied, stored in a retrieval system, or transmitted in any form or by any means without prior permission in writing from the copyright holder. Nor may it be otherwise circulated in any form or binding or cover other than the one in which it is published and without conditions including this condition being imposed on the subsequent purchaser.

ISBN 978-1-906198-02-2

Cover Design by Karen Cooper

Contents

Foreword

Way back in 1989 I was made redundant from Nokia and embarked on a new career as a freelance sales and marketing consultant. When I first started I had to force myself to go and talk to people at business events, because that was the best way to get work. Within a very short time I had mastered how to connect with strangers, engage them in conversation for three or four minutes, ask for their contact information and leave. But most importantly, I learned to keep my eyes open and grasp any opportunities to meet new people.

I had one of those life-changing moments when I met Liz. She was about thirty-six years old and I first saw her in early summer. She was wearing jeans, a black T-shirt and brown boots and was just about to step on the escalator in Selfridges. By chance I followed her down and when she got to the bottom I went up to her and said, 'Excuse me, your label's showing. Can I put it back?'

She laughed and said 'yes', so I did. We started to chat about clothes as her T-shirt was from a major fashion chain. After a few minutes I suggested that we have a coffee together and she agreed. We ended up talking for about half an hour. She was also self-employed and worked as a graphic designer. Six months later I started a marketing project for a major company with her partner, Neil.

That opened my eyes to the opportunities of meeting people in public places as opposed to business meetings, conferences, social events or parties.

Now I believe that every relationship – whether it's for business, for friendship, or for love – starts with a connection. And that connection can happen anywhere. As I repeatedly tell people, 'you don't know if the person behind you at the cash point queue is the one you're looking for. And the only way to find out is to turn round and talk to them.'

The trick is to grasp the moment and follow it up without any expectations or fear of rejection. And that's what this book is about. I have written it as a story, but it's based on actual incidents that have happened on my Flirting Safaris (www.flirtingsafari.com). I have run these for over five years and almost five hundred people have been on them in eight cities around the UK. Their feedback has convinced me that it's a much better way to meet a potential partner than in a bar or club. All I have done in this book is change names and locations to protect their privacy.

At the end of each chapter I've summarised the techniques which you need to put into practice. Practice makes perfect. And the more you practise, the more relaxed and confident you will become and the more successful you will be.

In this book I mention a number of retail chains and brands by name. In doing so I acknowledge that these are copyright trade names, but I use them for clarity and authenticity.

Peter Spalton
The Dating Doctor™
peter@spalton.co.uk

Chapter 1

On the Starting Line

Rita stood waiting on Davies Street outside the entrance to Bond Street tube. It was a grey Saturday in October and she was about to go on a Flirting Safari. Oxford Street had started to fill up with shoppers looking for bargains. There was a chill in the air so most of them were wearing their coats for the first time since the summer. She glanced at her watch, it was 11:15, and she looked round at the coffee shop behind her. But before she could decide, she saw a tall man in jeans and a dark jacket walking down the street towards her.

As he came closer she recognised him from the website and smiled. He stopped in front of her and said, 'Hi, I'm Robert, your dating coach.'

'Hello, I'm Rita. I thought I recognised you from your picture.'

'I'm sorry I wasn't here to meet you, but I've been checking out a place where we can have some coffee.'

'That's OK, I'm always early and I'm dying for a coffee. How many are coming today?'

'Five. Two men and two other women. It's a good number because you'll learn from watching each other and I'll be able to give you some individual coaching.'

Just then two others arrived within a few seconds of each other and introduced themselves; Adrian and Suzie. Rita said hello and they stood there chatting as they waited for the other two.

Robert studied the group as they talked amongst themselves. Rita must have been in her early fifties and looked a bit tired. She was wearing flatties, jeans, a black T-shirt and a leather jacket. Suzie was well dressed in trousers, a designer top and a lovely red coat; she was probably in her early forties. On the other hand, Adrian was in his early thirties and dressed in jeans and white trainers with a fleece zipped right up to the top. He had a rucksack slung over one shoulder.

Robert was doing what everyone else does – making judgements about people based on a first impression – how they dress, how they stand and how they sound.

Adrian turned to Robert and asked nervously, 'What actually are we going to be doing today?'

'I'll explain when the other two arrive,' he replied. 'They should be here in a bit and then we'll go for a coffee and a briefing.'

The next to arrive was Sukhon, a smartly dressed Asian woman in a skirt, cream jacket and designer handbag. She looked in her early thirties, but was probably about ten years older. Finally Edward, wearing black chinos, a white shirt, expensive-looking shoes and a blue jacket. He must have been in his late thirties.

Now that they were all here Robert asked them to introduce themselves by saying who they were and whereabouts they lived. It turned out that Suzie and Edward lived near each other in Battersea. She worked in banking and he was the sales manager for a computer company. Sukhon worked for an independent television company and lived near Notting Hill, whereas Rita lived in Clapham. Adrian had travelled the furthest as he lived in Maidenhead and worked in computer support for an insurance company.

Robert then began to explain what they were going to do. 'This afternoon we're going to talk to strangers.' They all looked worried as they realised it was about to start. 'I only have three objectives,' Robert continued. 'First, to open your eyes to the opportunities around you. Second, to teach you how to talk to strangers. And third, to have some fun.'

They laughed nervously as Robert carried on, 'We're going to hunt for people in the shops. And I want you to talk to as many as you can, without any expectations. Great, if it works out. If it doesn't, just shrug your shoulders and walk away. Say to yourself that if you don't have any expectations, you've got nothing to lose.'

They looked anxious and Adrian said, 'What if we meet someone we really like?'

'You ask for their phone number. I'll explain how to do that later. But first, let's go get a coffee and talk this through.' Turning, he then led them across the road and up Oxford Street to the narrow alley of St Christopher's Place. Not many tourists knew of this cut-through so it was reasonably quiet. In the sixties it used to be a red-light district, now it was full of designer shops and restaurants. He stopped outside the coffee shop where he'd already reserved a table.

Learning Points

- Over 90 percent of your first impression of someone is based on how they look (a combination of their dress and body language) and how they sound when they say 'hello.'

- Have no expectations so you can shrug off the fear of rejection.

Chapter 2

The Briefing

They ordered their drinks and drifted downstairs to sit nervously around a large table with a reserved sign. When they had all settled, Robert explained.

'Today, we're going to shop for people, not products. So I don't want any excuses like "I don't fancy him." We're talking to people for the sake of talking to them. So treat everyone you meet as though they are attractive, interesting and single. Later you might find out that they're none of those, but that doesn't matter. The point is to practise so when you meet someone you really fancy you'll come across as confident and relaxed.'

They looked very apprehensive, but he continued. 'Remember, we're shopping for people so please don't buy anything. And, we need to hunt for people where they'll be browsing and happy to talk to you.'

'What do you mean?' Edward interrupted.

'Somewhere they've got time. Places like art galleries, railway stations, airports, bookshops and supermarkets,' Robert replied and went on to explain that the big supermarkets were good for three reasons.

'First, they have a trolley and can't escape. Second, there are lots of things on the shelves to talk about. And finally, the stuff in their trolley tells you about their lifestyle. So if they've got cat food, they probably have a cat or two.'

Suzie interjected, 'Oh, and dinner for one and half a bottle of champagne.'

The group laughed and Robert went on, 'The hardest part is to keep the conversation going for a few minutes after you've said hello. The trick is to use your eyes and ears and latch onto what we call free information, in this case the things in their trolley.'

He paused and looked at each of them in turn. 'Bookshops are also very good. Upmarket ones like Waterstone's with carpets, lots of space between the aisles and chairs. On a Safari last year one of the women in the group got chatting to a guy in the travel section and they ended up having a coffee together on the top floor. She caught up with us twenty minutes later. At the other end of the spectrum are places like WH Smith, which is a family shop.'

Robert looked at the girls and carried on. 'If you want to hunt for men you should go to gadget shops. You'll see them standing in front of a television, a computer screen or a rack of MP3 players with their mouths open. All you have to do is slide up beside them and say something like, "a nice screen, isn't it?" They'll reply along the lines of, "No, it's LCD, I think plasma's better".'

Suzie winced and interrupted, 'I could never say anything as corny as that.'

'I know it sounds corny but, as you'll discover, it almost doesn't matter what you say. What's important is how you look and how you sound. In the seventies an American professor, Albert Mehrabian, did some research that measured what determines whether we like someone or not when we first meet them. Interestingly, how you look accounts for 55 percent, how you sound 38 percent and what you say is only 7 percent.' Robert glanced round the group and continued, 'So the chat-up line doesn't really matter. But if you think "nice screen" is too corny, you could always ask their advice about choosing an iPod.'

'But what if I don't want an iPod?' Rita asked.

'Then pretend you're buying one as a birthday gift. Remember this is about meeting people, not buying things.'

'I read somewhere that people love being asked their advice,' interjected Edward.

'Yes, they see it as a great compliment, so exploit it.' Robert paused and looked at the girls who were all sitting together. 'You'll also find men browsing in outdoor shops. The serious ones like Ellis & Bingham, Mountain Shack and Snow & Rock. Avoid Millets as it's mainly for families and Blacks is men with teenage sons. At this time of the year the guys will be going out in pairs to buy their snowboarding boots, ski goggles and ice climbing gear.'

Robert then turned to Adrian and Edward. 'If you want to meet girls, don't go into clothes or shoe shops because they won't be interested in you. Women browse for things like chocolates, jams and pickles, candles and ornaments and what I call cards and bows. Go and hunt in places like the food sections of department stores or shops like Habitat, Paperchase, Lush and WH Smith. Avoid Clinton Cards as it's usually full of teenagers buying furry toys and gushing cards for their mother or boyfriend.'

He looked at each of them in turn as he was talking to check that they were taking it all in. 'Unfortunately we can't do all those today. But we are going to hunt in a bookshop, a gadget shop, a cook shop and a record shop.' Robert paused for a couple of seconds and said, 'Do any of you have any questions?'

They looked nervously at the floor so he went on, 'OK, first we'll do a warm-up in the perfume section of Selfridges where I want you to talk to shop assistants. It's very easy to start a conversation with them, all you have to do is catch their eye and smile. They will probably say "hello". If they don't, just stop in front of them and say "hi". Then what I want you to do is turn the conversation onto personal things like where they live, their holidays and so on. The trick is to talk about what interests them, not what you're into.

'They will be happy to talk about their work (what they're doing at the moment), where they live, what they did on holiday or last weekend and what's going on in the world (such as the weather). But shop assistants on commission will always bring it back to the product because that's their livelihood. So use your eyes and ears – listen for an accent and if they don't seem to be from London, ask them where they're from. If they're very young this might be a Saturday job, so ask them about university. If they're wearing anything interesting, ask them about it. Some have printed T-shirts, others will have a nice pendant, necklace or pair of earrings. You should give them a compliment by pointing to it and saying something like, "that's lovely, where did you get it?" But only compliment them on their possessions, not how they look.'

They looked a bit confused and Edward said, 'So I can't mention her eyes.'

'That's right. As a man I think that's too personal. Although a woman would probably get away with asking about her hair. It's always safer to give them a compliment about what they own or what they're doing, rather than personal things like their hair, eyes or figure. Although you can mention their tan and use it as an opener by saying something like "you look as though you've had a great holiday."'

They all nodded and he said, 'If you've no more questions, let's go.' They remained silent so he stood up with, 'And whatever you do, please don't buy anything.' Turning to the girls, he added, 'And if you go for the free make-up session, we'll leave you.'

Learning Points

- Keep your eyes open and learn to shop for people rather than products.

- Go where people are browsing and have the time to talk to you. Try and get in the habit of starting a conversation with anyone within three feet. Wherever you are.

- Talk about the things that interest them, not the ones you're interested in. Generally they will be happy to talk about five things: what they are doing at that moment; why they're there; where they live; their holidays and interests; and what's going on in the world.

- What you say to start a conversation is not as important as how you sound and look when you say it. Look calm, confident and relaxed and speak in a slow, soft and friendly voice.

- Only give sincere compliments about a stranger's possessions or what they are doing. It's not appropriate to make personal comments such as 'that hair style really suits you'.

Chapter 3

Picking up the Scent

With Adrian at his side, Robert led them up the back road that ran parallel to Oxford Street towards Selfridges. Everyone else held back and walked slowly about ten yards behind. Although Adrian seemed very brash and brave, he told Robert that he had a terrible fear of rejection. Robert explained that most women also have that fear but it manifests in a different way. 'If they meet a guy they really fancy they get scared of making a fool of themselves. They get very nervous and either talk very fast in a babble, or get tongue-tied.'

They stopped outside the main entrance to Selfridges with its imposing bronze doors and waited for the others to catch up. When they'd gathered around he reiterated what they were going to do. 'We're going to talk to the perfume girls as a warm-up. They're very easy to talk to as all you have to do is smile at them and say hello.'

'Yes,' said Edward, 'but most of them are pretty stunning. I never know where to look, especially if they're wearing a low-cut top.'

'Try and look at their face,' Robert replied. 'Their whole face, not just their eyes or mouth. The worst thing you can do is look away. That sends a signal that you're not interested in them and it doesn't help you concentrate on what they're saying.' He continued, 'Remember what I said about free information – notice what they're wearing, listen to their accent and make a stab at how they're feeling. And use that to change the direction of your conversation.'

'That's going to be difficult,' commented Rita. 'I'm a scent addict.'

'Yes, it's hardest for the women,' he said, looking at Rita, Sukhon and Suzie in turn. 'But if they try and force you to buy something, ask for a sample and explain that you'll come back later. Don't forget this is only a warm-up. Most of the time shop assistants will be happy to break the monotony of work and chat to someone like you. They will only insist on talking product if their manager is watching. You'll be surprised by the sort of things they will tell you if you're more interested in them than their product.'

Suzie interrupted, 'I suppose the secret is just to be friendly?'

'Absolutely,' said Robert. 'You need to look open, friendly and approachable. Not freaky. Before you go into any shop undo your coat, loosen your scarf and take your hands out of your pockets so you have an open posture. Stand tall with your head up as though you are walking into a room full of gorgeous people.'

As he demonstrated, Robert appeared to grow by an extra inch or two. He paused and continued, 'Put the angel on your shoulder rather than the devil. And imagine that the angel whispers in your ear "you are looking good and you can do this," as you walk slowly and purposefully through the door.'

Turning to Adrian he said, 'That rucksack will cause a problem with your posture because you'll lean forward to compensate for the weight. So you won't appear to stand tall.'

Adrian nodded and took it off. Robert held out his hand and said, 'Let me carry it for you while we do this.'

Adrian passed it over and replied, 'I never thought about that, thanks.'

With that Robert looked at his watch and said, 'Please stay in the perfume section so I can find you and we'll meet back out here in fifteen minutes.' He turned, opened the door and swung his arm to invite them to enter the shop. They apprehensively went though the open door one by one – like lambs to the slaughter.

Rita was the last to enter and Robert slid alongside her. Out of the corner of his eye he saw Edward approach one of the girls at the Agent Provocateur counter. She was wearing a white lab coat unbuttoned to the waist to show off her red bra. Robert smiled as he saw Edward struggle to keep his eyes on her face.

Turning to Rita he said, 'Let's walk slowly and find someone for you to talk to. The easiest are the girls at the end of the aisles with a bottle of perfume and the test strips.' He pointed to a young Asian girl at the end of an aisle and said, 'Why don't you go and talk to her?'

'If I must,' Rita replied nervously.

'Remember to move the conversation into personal things.'

'I will,' she said as she started to walk reluctantly up to the young girl.

Robert hung back and watched her out of the corner of his eye. She seemed to stand a bit too far away from the girl. It's always best to be about an arm's length from the other person and almost facing them straight on. But as she seemed to be getting on all right, he turned away and went to look for the others.

He walked slowly, standing tall with his head held high just like he'd told them. He came across Adrian on the edge of the perfume section just as he parted company with a tall blonde on the Origins Organics counter. 'How did you get on?' he asked.

'Better than I thought,' he replied. 'She's from Germany and been here for about a year.'

'Well done. Did you learn anything else?'

'Yes, she's got this idea for an internet business selling specialist creams and is working here to get more experience. Apparently Origins stuff is good.'

'I don't know about that, but you did well,' Robert said, touching Adrian gently on his upper arm. 'Why don't you try someone else while I look for the others. I'll see you outside in five minutes or so.'

'OK,' said Adrian, checking the time on his mobile.

Robert continued his walk and saw Suzie wandering rather aimlessly. He speeded up and came alongside her. 'How are you doing, Suzie?'

'Not so well, I'm afraid. I spoke to one girl over there but I can't seem to switch the conversation to personal stuff. She just wanted to sell me things.'

'It's not easy,' Robert replied. 'The best way is to use your eyes and ears to take in the free information. If you see anything that seems interesting or unusual, just pursue it.' He glanced around and spied a shop assistant who looked Turkish or Greek. 'Why don't you try her, she doesn't look like a Londoner,' he suggested.

'OK,' she replied with a laugh and walked slowly towards the girl that Robert had pointed out.

Robert watched her for a minute and then walked around the area to look for the others. After a couple of minutes he looked at his watch and wandered outside to where Sukhon and Edward were chatting. The others arrived within half a minute and crowded in a semi-circle around Robert. He asked them how they'd got on and listened as they talked about their experiences. Apart from Sukhon, they were more relaxed and almost buzzing. Robert made a mental note to stick with Sukhon in the bookshop.

Learning Points

- Look open, friendly and approachable by undoing your coat, taking your hands out of your pockets and standing tall.

- Walk slowly with purpose and your head held high.

- Don't think too hard about what you're going to say. Use your eyes and ears to gather free information and start the conversation. Things like what they are doing, wearing and maybe feeling.

- Stand about an arm's length away from the other person and almost facing them – about seventeen degrees.

- Look at the other person's face when they're talking so you appear to be interested in what they are saying.

- Everyone has a fear of rejection at some time or another. Remind yourself that it's much better to have tried than to regret doing nothing.

Chapter 4

Through the Barrier

When their chatter about the perfume girls began to dwindle Robert gently interrupted and pointed to Waterstone's on the other side of Oxford Street. 'In a couple of minutes we'll go to the bookshop and do it for real.' Their smiles dropped onto the pavement, and he continued, 'It's only two floors but I want you to talk to customers. When you spot someone, stand back and study the situation they're in. Ask yourself what sort of book are they looking at, what's the best side to approach them, and is there anything unusual about where they are or what they're doing?'

'But what can we say?' asked Rita.

'Let me answer that in a bit. First, you need to understand how to approach them,' Robert replied. 'Walk slowly up beside them, stop and look at the shelves for a second or two. Turn your body towards them in a big movement so they catch it out of the corner of their eye. Then speak in an assertive voice. They need to know that you're talking to them and not muttering into your phone or talking to yourself.'

'You make it sound easy,' said Edward. 'What happens if they ignore us?'

'Then either walk away or repeat what you said a little louder,' answered Robert.

And he continued, 'As far as what to say, don't think about it too much. It's best to be spontaneous. Make a comment about what they're doing or the situation you're both in. Something like "are you planning to go to New Zealand?" (if that's what they're reading about), or "that's a great book" as you point to what they're looking at. If you see someone hovering at the three-for-two pile you could say "I can never find three I like either".'

They all laughed nervously and he went on, 'As we walk around I'll give you some other ideas. Please don't pick up a book as you will be tempted to open it hoping it will tell you what to say, I can assure you it won't.'

Just then one of the security guards came out of Selfridges and gave them a funny look. Robert pointed over the road and they followed him as he walked towards the traffic lights.

He stopped outside Waterstone's and waited. When they'd all caught up he explained that the travel section was one of the easiest. 'Generally you'll find women in alternative health, popular psychology, and mind, body and spirit. Men, on the other hand, are often in cookery, sport and computers.' He stepped back and waved them into the shop saying, 'Now go for it. We'll meet back out here in 20 minutes. And remember if you pick up a book, don't open it.'

Sukhon was looking very awkward and Robert murmured, 'How are you feeling, Sukhon?'

'Not good,' she replied.

'It's not easy. This is the most scary thing for just about everyone. But when you get through the first one, you'll wonder what all the fuss was about.'

'It's just that I'm not sure I can do it,' she nervously replied.

Robert started to walk to the stairs and said, 'Let's try the travel section downstairs.' She walked slowly beside him with her head down and Robert gently prodded her, saying, 'Head up and shoulders back.'

When they reached the bottom he pointed towards a man browsing a book by the Europe rack. 'You see him?'

'Yes,' she replied anxiously.

'Go alongside, look at the rack for a few seconds and then turn to him and ask if he's seen a book on Florence.'

'Isn't that a bit cheeky?'

'Not really, just be friendly. But when he passes you the book, say "thank you" and just look at the cover. Don't open it.'

'OK, then what?'

'That's easy, just ask him what's he's looking at, listen to his reply and use that as the thread of your conversation. He'll quite happily talk about what he's doing now and why.'

'It can't be as easy as that,' she said in a sceptical tone.

'It is. The worst that can happen is he just grunts or ignores you. If he does, count slowly to five and then calmly walk away.'

Robert moved out of sight and watched her gingerly walk over to the man. She did as he'd suggested and Robert smiled when he saw the man pick a book from the shelf and hand it to her. He continued to watch for half a minute as they started to talk to each other before walking away to look for the others.

Meanwhile, Adrian had been talking to a tall Swedish girl in the alternative health section when the conversation seemed to die away. But he must have remembered what Robert had said about talking about their interests not your own because when he asked her about Stockholm her face lit up. She enthusiastically told him about the old part of the city and all the romantic little islands just off the coast.

Robert continued to wander and spotted Edward and Suzie chatting out of the way in a corner of the business section. When they spotted him they broke off and started to look for other people to talk to. Robert collared Suzie and asked how she was doing.

'Not bad,' she replied. 'I spoke to a guy in the cookery section and he almost immediately told me he was looking for a present for his wife.'

'I expect that changed the whole dynamics of the conversation,' Robert replied.

'Yes, it did. I was much more relaxed, and so was he. We talked about Italian cooking which was both our favourites. He is a nice guy,' she said, almost with regret.

At that moment a beaming Sukhon came over to join them. She'd been through the pain barrier and told Suzie all about the guy in the travel section. Robert made a mental note to tell Sukhon she ought to put her hair up so she'd stop fiddling with it when she was nervous. He quietly left them to it and walked up the stairs to the ground floor.

There Rita was prowling amongst the fiction books and about to talk to a man browsing in the three-for-two pile. Robert watched her from behind a counter for a minute or two, looked at his watch and went outside to meet the others.

Everyone apart from Rita had gathered in a group bragging about who they'd talked to and how they'd got on. You could see that they were excited from the adrenalin. Rita soon joined them and told the others how she'd done with the guy at the three-for-two pile. 'He was a fantasy addict and told me how he loved to read about castles and warriors in unknown lands.'

'I spoke to him downstairs in mind, body and spirit,' interjected Suzie.

'He must have thought his luck was in. Chatted up by two girls within ten minutes,' grinned Edward.

'Yes,' responded Rita, 'I was surprised how people were happy to talk and really open up. But I did feel a bit awkward when I asked a guy if he could suggest a book as a present for my brother. Especially when I don't have one.'

'I don't see that as a problem,' said Robert. 'You're not doing any harm and if you end up with a date you can always tell him and laugh over it.'

'I have one question,' said Sukhon, turning to Robert. 'One of the guys I approached got very nervous when I started talking to him. He rubbed his hands and kept looking around. I thought he was going to run off in fright.'

'I suspect that his partner was also in the shop,' replied Robert. 'He wouldn't want her to see him chatting you up.'

They all laughed and Robert moved them on by saying, 'Now let's go back to Selfridges and play on the lower ground floor.'

Learning Points

- Don't think too hard about what you're going to say. Take in everything they're doing and notice anything that seems unusual or interesting. Wait no longer than three seconds before you speak.

- When you're standing beside them, turn towards them with a big movement and then speak in an assertive voice.

- You can only open a conversation in one of three ways – make a statement or comment, ask a question, or make a statement followed by a question. The classic openers are to say hello (hi, how are you doing?), to ask their advice (can you see a book on a Florence?), or to make a comment about the situation you're both in (I can never find three I like either).

- Keep the conversation going by using free information. Check out what they're wearing, looking at, doing, saying and feeling.

- Talk about their interests, not your own.

- Try not to fiddle with your clothes, jewellery or hair when you get nervous.

- Only pick up a product to use it as a prop. Never ever open a book.

- Don't worry if their partner is in the shop. You'll soon know from the way they respond to you.

- If they're married or in a serious relationship, they will usually tell you in some way or another. When that happens the dynamics of the conversation will completely change and you'll both talk like friends.

Chapter 5

On a Roll

Robert led them back across Oxford Street and through the corner entrance to Selfridges. Suzie and Sukhon stopped a couple of times to drool over the handbags as they followed him to the down-escalator. They formed a circle around Robert at the bottom.

When they had settled down he told them where they were going to play. 'There's a large technology section through the books over there,' he said as he pointed to the right. 'On the left is a Muji concession which sells what I call gifts and bows for girls. You'll find that they pick them up just like they do with books, so you have plenty of time to approach them. Of course you'll find the boys just staring with their mouths open at the technology stuff.'

'I shall go and hunt for men amongst the gadgets,' interrupted Suzie. 'I might even try out your "nice screen" opener,' she said with a cheeky grin.

'Great,' responded Robert. 'But before you do that let me tell you about the other areas you can hunt.' Pointing ahead he continued, 'Through there are ornaments and candles, a cook-shop and a small art gallery. Behind us is luggage, which is also quite good. You just have to ask them where they're going.'

'What about foods and chocolates? Jams and pickles, I think you called them,' asked Adrian.

'Yes, that's where you'll find women. It's on the other side of the cook-shop,' replied Robert. 'But before you all rush off, let me give you a couple of extra tips.'

Robert then went on to explain that the best way to keep the conversation going is to listen intently to what they are telling you. 'Follow the thread of what they are talking about and make comments or ask them open questions about it.' He then added, 'Remember some of the other things they have mentioned so you can use them to restart the conversation when it begins to fall flat. The important thing to remember is that if you listen, they will tell you what to say.'

They all nodded intently and he carried on, 'If you really get on well with them you must ask for their phone number. The best way to do that is what I call CIA – compliment, intent and ask. So give them a compliment such as "I really enjoyed talking to you about...", state your intent with "I'd like to meet you again" and ask "can I have your number?"'

'You always make it sound so easy,' said Edward.

'Believe me, it is,' replied Robert. 'I know it's easy for me to say, but your fear of rejection is just in your head. Repeat to yourself "it's better to do something, than regret doing nothing" and if you don't ask you've got nothing.'

They nodded so he continued, 'Let's go and hunt for people and meet back here in about 45 minutes. Then we'll all go to the music store.'

Adrian looked at his phone and the rest of them glanced at their watches. They nodded and slowly drifted off. Suzie and Sukhon towards technology, Rita to books and Edward to gifts and bows where he'd already spied a couple of stunning girls. Robert turned to Adrian and said, 'Let's go to the cook-shop.'

Suzie and Sukhon walked slowly and purposefully through the book section as Robert had shown them. It was like a rabbit warren and opened out into an enormous space crammed with big-screen TVs, drum kits, gaming consoles, laptops, digital cameras and mobile phones. 'Boys' toys,' Sukhon commented sarcastically.

Meanwhile Robert and Adrian wandered though the ornaments section looking for women to talk to. Adrian stopped, turned to Robert and said, 'I'm not sure that I have the guts to ask for a phone number.'

'Yes, it is hard. But just remember that the worst that can happen is she gives you a bum number.'

'What do you mean?' asked Adrian.

'Women will often change the last digit of their phone number rather than say no. If she gives you a number, don't dial it in front of her as it says you don't trust her. A bum number is the worst thing, but if you don't ask you'll probably regret it for a long time.'

'Yes, I suppose you're right. Is it any easier for women?'

'Well, I suppose that most guys will give a women their number. But women have the same fear of hurt and rejection.'

'And I thought it was only men who were nervous,' commented Adrian.

Just then Robert spotted two girls looking at the candles on a centre island and said, 'Why don't you go and talk to those two girls? But treat them both the same otherwise the one that you ignore will block you from her friend.'

'Hmm, I'll try. Then can I go to the food section?'

'Yeah. I'll see you back at the escalator in half an hour,' said Robert as Adrian started to walk towards the two girls. He watched as Adrian said something to them and they both responded with a laugh. 'Nicely done,' thought Robert and turned round to find the others.

Meanwhile Suzie had left Sukhon and gone to talk to a guy staring at the digital cameras. She'd opened the conversation and now they seemed to be getting on like a house on fire. Sukhon had watched for a few seconds, jealous of the other's go-for-it attitude. She then wandered off to look at the flat-screen televisions. There were a few men standing and staring just as Robert had predicted. Eventually she plucked up the courage to approach a not-so-good-looking guy and said meekly, 'Nice screen, isn't it?'

He turned to look at her and replied, 'Yeah, but it's the sound that's really good,' before going on to explain about high definition.

Sukhon tried not to look too bored and managed to turn the conversation onto where he was from and why he was in town. Surprisingly they chatted together for about five minutes before the conversation died and she said goodbye.

Meanwhile Robert had drifted into the art gallery and bumped into Rita. 'I'm not really into contemporary art,' he told her.

'Me neither,' she replied and she went on to tell him she was a widow and still in love with her dead husband. 'My daughter is now eighteen and has told me to do something about it and find a Mr Almost Right.'

'She's right,' responded Robert. 'You need to move on and stop comparing every man you meet with your husband. He probably wouldn't want you to grieve for ever.'

As they walked back to the meeting place they continued to talk about how she'd have to kiss a lot of frogs, as well as a few toads. By the time they got back most of the group was already waiting. Edward and Suzie ambled along deep in conversation about two minutes later. When they'd clustered round, Robert asked, 'How did you all get on?'

'I really enjoyed that,' said Sukhon. 'I spoke to a couple of guys in technology.' She paused and then said, 'Tell you what, I shall be back here next Saturday to hunt for some more.'

Suzie responded to Robert's glance with, 'I got on really well with a guy telling me all about digital cameras. I didn't know they were so complicated. But I got his number.' She waved a bit of paper and gave Edward a sly smile. Everyone grinned and Sukhon said, 'Fantastic, well done.'

Adrian and Edward looked at the floor and Robert congratulated her.

'I bumped into a man that I'd already spoken to in the bookshop,' interjected Rita. 'And I jokingly accused him of following me.'

Suzie laughed and Robert interrupted the banter by asking them if they now understood how people went about their shopping.

'Yes,' said Edward. 'I was fascinated to see how they browsed differently in each of the various departments.'

'They do,' added Robert. 'Now we're going to see how they do it in the CD and DVD shop. Then we'll go to the pub for a drink and recap.' He went on to explain that a music store was entirely different for two reasons. First, there wasn't much free information to help them – it might just say Rock A to Z. Second, people don't stop for very long because there's not much to read on the back of a CD or DVD. 'After all,' he said, 'it's not like a book. You will have to move in fast if you want to talk to them.'

'Umm,' muttered Rita, 'and I suppose the background music doesn't actually help either.'

'True,' replied Robert. 'It's just like a club or bar. But at least it doesn't have the implicit pick-up agenda that they do.' With that, he handed the rucksack back to Adrian and led the group slowly towards the music section. When they arrived at the entrance he told them to meet him outside in ten minutes.

Learning Points

- If you speak to two people together, treat them the same and let them make the choice.

- Even though you're nervous, try not to talk too fast.

- Ask for a phone number with CIA. Give a compliment, state your intent and ask for their number.

- If you listen, they will tell you what to say.

- You have to kiss a lot of frogs before you find The One.

- There is an implicit pick-up agenda in bars and clubs. This doesn't happen when you talk to strangers in shops, railway stations or art galleries.

Chapter 6

Recap and Relax

They looked tired, but buzzing with excitement, as they sat round a table upstairs in the pub. When they'd all settled with a drink, Robert raised his glass and said, 'Well done, everyone. I can see you enjoyed it and I hope that you learnt a lot.'

'Thank you,' they all replied almost in unison and Suzie continued, 'I nearly got cold feet this morning and didn't turn up. But I'm glad I did. It's the best thing I've done for ages.'

Robert grinned in appreciation and asked if they had any questions.

'Just one,' said Adrian. 'What's the best way to end the conversation and walk away?'

'It's called breaking out,' replied Robert. 'You need to break out on a high before the conversation starts to drag. You want to leave them with the feeling that they'd like to talk to you again. As the conversation starts to drag give a reason, say goodbye and leave as soon as you can. For instance, you could look at your watch and say something like "I better go, I was meant to meet my mates five minutes ago." Then stay another half minute so you don't appear to be keen to rush off.'

They nodded and Adrian asked, 'How long should you wait before you call them?'

'Well, you don't want to seem desperate. So, personally I'd say 24 hours and not later than 2 days.'

The group began to relax and fell silent so Robert said, 'I'll leave you in a bit to catch my train. But before I go, let me remind you of three key points. First, talk to everyone within three feet and treat them as though they are attractive, interesting and single.' He looked around the group and they nodded. 'Second, take your iPod out and look available. Walk slowly with an open posture and purpose. And finally, try and read their body language so you get a feel for what they think about you.'

After a few more minutes of general chatter, Robert said goodbye and left them to talk about the day amongst themselves.

The following evening he got an email from Suzie.

Hi Robert

It's Suzie from the flirting safari yesterday. I was looking for a confidence boost and it certainly worked. It was great fun and now I must keep practising.

You may have noticed that Edward and I got on really well, but I was disappointed that he never asked me for my number. Could you ask him if you can give me his email address?

Thanks again, Suzie

Robert sat back in his chair and thought, 'why do men always seem to misread or ignore the signals?'

Learning Points

- Break out before the conversation drags. Give a reason, say bye and go.

- Switch off your iPod and walk with an open and friendly posture so you look available. You'll be surprised what happens.

- Grasp the moment. Talk to everyone within three feet and remember it's better to do something than regret doing nothing.

- Try and read their body language when you talk to them so you get a feel for what they think about you.

Chapter 7

A Dozen Big Thoughts

1 Walk SLOWLY with your HEAD UP, be relaxed and notice things around you.

2 Treat EVERYONE you meet as though they are attractive, interesting and single.

3 Look CONFIDENT and RELAXED with your hands out of your pockets.

4 Don't think too hard about what you're going to say. Use your eyes and ears to get FREE INFORMATION to start the conversation.

5 When you're standing beside them, speak within THREE SECONDS. Turn towards them with a big movement and then speak in an assertive voice.

6 Always look at their FACE when they're talking so you appear to be interested in what they are saying. Stand almost facing them at about SEVENTEEN degrees.

7 Talk about the things that INTEREST THEM, not the ones you're interested in.

8   If you LISTEN they will tell you what to say.

9   Try not to FIDDLE with your clothes, jewellery or hair as you look nervous. Only pick up a product to use it as a prop. Never ever open a book.

10 Ask for a phone number before the conversation starts to die. Use CIA – COMPLIMENT, state your INTENT and ASK for their number.

11 Talk to everyone within three feet – remember it's better to DO SOMETHING than regret doing nothing.

12 Always GRASP THE MOMENT and just see where it leads. You will be surprised.

For Your Notes

About The Author

Peter Spalton aka The Dating Doctor has a talent to help people of both sexes build their confidence and create lasting relationships. He is a widely recognised relationship guru in the field of social skills, flirting, dating, seduction and body language. He provides personal coaching as well as flirting, dating and seduction workshops around the British Isles.

Peter has worked in sales and marketing for 28 years and frequently gives expert advice to newspapers and magazines for articles that relate to a whole host of issues to do with flirting, dating, seduction and body language. He is a member of the advisory board to the Academy of Sex and Relationships in London and the media have given him labels like the 'Body Boffin', 'Dating Guru' and 'Love Coach'. He is heard on two to three radio slots around the country every month and has featured on national and local television. He has been married for 23 years and lives near Worcester, England.

You can get the Dating Doctor's Tips on Flirting and other books as well as help on how to find your one at www.thedatingdoctor.co.uk